CGP has Year 3 Spelling practice covered!

The best way for pupils to improve their Spelling in Year 3 (ages 7-8) is by doing as much practice as they can.

That's where this book comes in. It's packed with questions that'll test them on all the crucial Spelling skills, including those introduced for the first time in Year 3.

And there's more! Everything is perfectly matched to the National Curriculum and we've included answers at the back. Enjoy!

What CGP is all about

Our sole aim here at CGP is to produce the highest quality books — carefully written, immaculately presented and dangerously close to being funny.

Then we work our socks off to get them out to you — at the cheapest possible prices.

Published by CGP

Editors
Keith Blackhall, Heather Cowley, Catherine Heygate, Gabrielle Richardson, Hayley Shaw, Sam Summers
With thanks to Andy Cashmore for the proofreading.
With thanks to Jan Greenway for the copyright research.

ISBN: 978 1 78294 127 9

Clipart from Corel®
Printed by Elanders Ltd, Newcastle upon Tyne.
Based on the classic CGP style created by Richard Parsons.

Text, design, layout and original illustrations © Coordination Group Publications Ltd. (CGP) 2022
All rights reserved.

Photocopying this book is not permitted, even if you have a CLA licence.
Extra copies are available from CGP with next day delivery • 0800 1712 712 • www.cgpbooks.co.uk

Contents

Section 1 – Prefixes

Prefixes — 'un', 'dis' and 'mis' 4
Prefixes — 're' and 'anti' 6
Prefixes — 'sub' and 'super' 7

Section 2 – Suffixes and Word Endings

Suffixes — 'ing' and 'ed' 8
Suffixes — 'er' and 'est' 10
Suffixes — 'ment', 'ness', 'ful' and 'less' 12
Suffixes — 'ation' and 'ous' 14
Suffixes — 'ly' 16
Word Endings — 'sure' and 'ture' 18

Section 3 – Confusing Words

The Short 'i' Sound 20
The Hard 'c' Sound 21
The Soft 'c' Sound 22
The 'sh' Sound 23
The 'ay' Sound 24
Word Families 25
Plurals 26
Possessive Apostrophes 28
Homophones 30

Section 4 – Mixed Spelling Practice

Mixed Spelling Practice 32

Spelling Hints and Tips 35
Answers 36

Section 1 — Prefixes

Prefixes – 'un', 'dis' and 'mis'

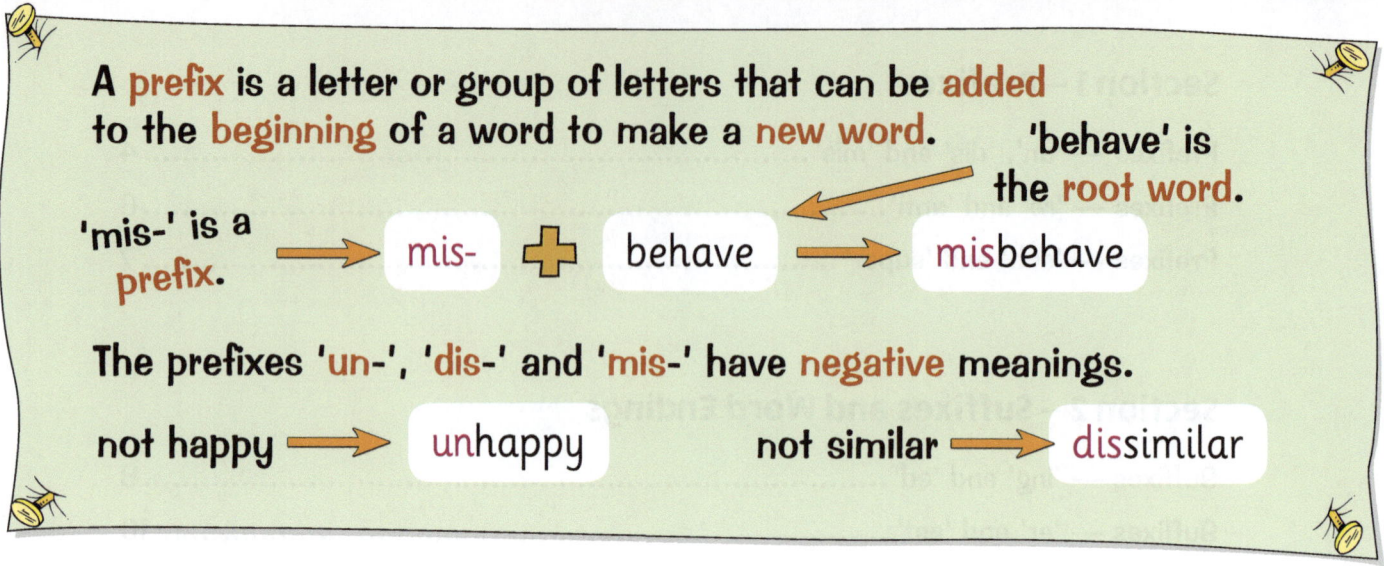

A prefix is a letter or group of letters that can be added to the beginning of a word to make a new word.

'mis-' is a prefix. → mis- + behave → misbehave

'behave' is the root word.

The prefixes 'un-', 'dis-' and 'mis-' have negative meanings.

not happy → unhappy   not similar → dissimilar

1 Split the words below into <u>prefixes</u> and <u>root</u> words.

unknown → .... + ...

misprint → .... + ...

disapprove → .... + ...

uneven → .... + ...

2 Add <u>un-</u>, <u>dis-</u> or <u>mis-</u> to spell the words below correctly. Then write the words out <u>in full</u>.

..............aware → ....

..............equal → ....

..............regard → ....

..............paid → ....

..............behave → ....

3) Underline the words below that have the wrong prefixes. Then write the correct spellings on the dotted lines.

unable   dislike   diskind   discalculate   unspell   misappoint

....
....
....
....

4) Draw lines from the prefixes to the correct root words.

dis-   mis-

own   miss   treat   please   match   agree

Write the completed words in the box.

5) Complete the words in these sentences using un-, dis- or mis-.

Asha went to hospital last night because she was very .... well.

Joanne left her car .... locked because the lock was broken.

The magician stepped inside the box and then .... appeared.

Pascal .... understood the question and got the answer wrong.

When we got to the hotel, we .... packed and ran to the pool.

Now Try This — Can you use each word from question 1 in a sentence?

Section 1 — Prefixes

Prefixes – 're' and 'anti'

The prefix 're-' means 'again' or 'back' when you add it to a root word.

reappear ⟵ 'reappear' means 'to appear again'

The prefix 'anti' means 'not' or 'against' when you add it to a root word.

'antisocial' means 'not sociable' ⟶ antisocial

1 Add re- or anti- to finish each word correctly.

..............clockwise   ....septic   ....charge

..............fresh   ....write   ....climax

..............create   ....heat   ....design

2 Draw lines from the prefixes to the correct root words.

Write the completed words in the box.

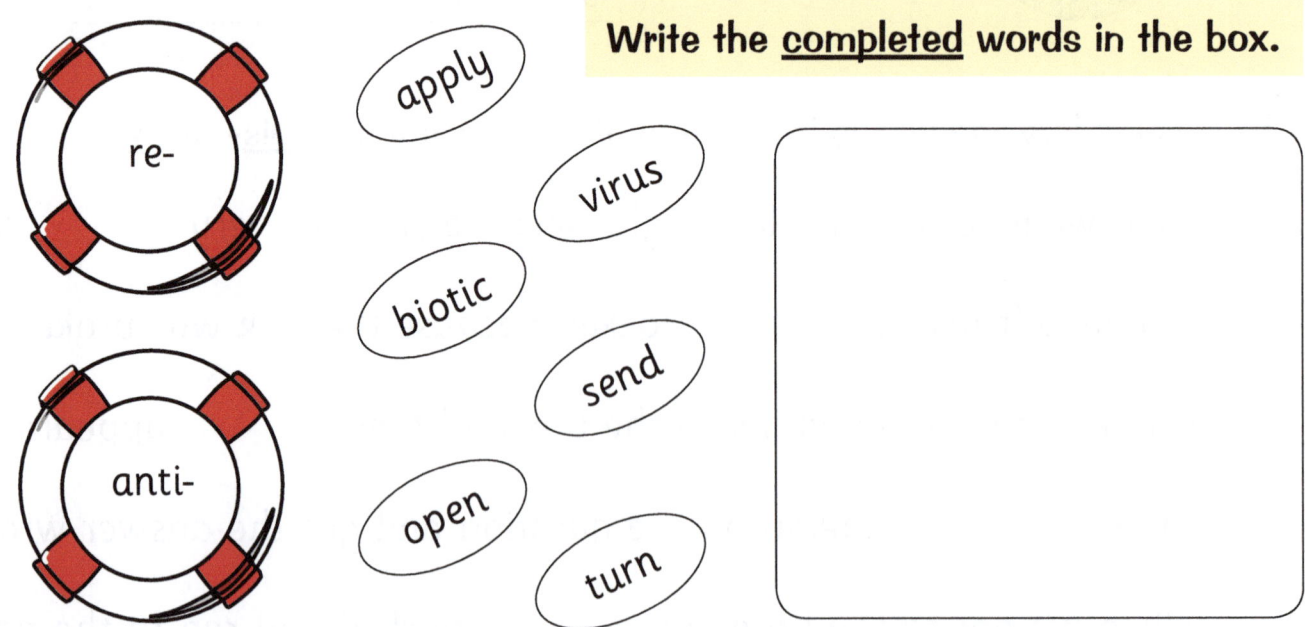

Now Try This "I built an enormous gingerbread house." How does the meaning of this sentence change when you add the prefix 're-' to the word 'built'?

Section 1 — Prefixes

Prefixes – 'sub' and 'super'

The prefix 'sub-' means 'under' when you add it to a root word.

subway ⟵ 'subway' means 'under the way'.

The prefix 'super' means 'above' or 'more than' when you add it to a root word.

'superstar' means 'a very successful person'. ⟶ superstar

1) Circle the correct spelling of each noun to complete the sentences.

The supermarine / submarine can reach depths of 300 feet.

Rupert stuck his fingers together with superglue / subglue.

Eren hates going to the supermarket / submarket on Saturdays.

The brave superhero / subhero came to the city's rescue.

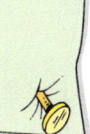

2) Complete the words in these sentences using sub- or super-.

My sandwich fell into the river and began to ....merge.

The train whizzed past at ....sonic speed.

The class was ....divided into three groups of ten people.

Lily didn't understand what each ....heading meant.

3) Write as many words as you can that start with each of these prefixes.

super-..

sub-..

 Use as many words from question 3 as you can in a single sentence.

Section 2 — Suffixes and Word Endings

Suffixes – 'ing' and 'ed'

A **suffix** is a letter or group of letters that can be **added** to the **end** of a word to make a **new word**.

'**clean**' is the **root word**. → clean + -ing → cleaning

'**-ing**' is a **suffix**.

Sometimes the spelling of the **root** word **doesn't change** when the suffixes '**-ing**' or '**-ed**' are added.

1) Add the <u>suffixes</u> to the root words and then write the words out in <u>full</u>.

hunt- + -ing / -ed → ....

jump- + -ing / -ed → ....

treat- + -ing / -ed → ....

2) Add <u>-ing</u> or <u>-ed</u> to the sentences below so that they make sense.

Ishra enjoys perform........ in plays at the theatre.

The clown entertain........ the children at the village fair.

The postman is deliver........ letters and parcels to Mr MacDonald.

Sometimes the spelling of the root word changes when the suffixes '-ing' or '-ed' are added.

The 'y' in 'marry' changes to 'i'.

marry + -ed → married

3) Circle the correct spelling of each word to complete the sentences.

Ben is out shoping / shopping with Nancy.

I am struggleing / struggling to do my homework.

Sometimes a letter is doubled when '-ing' or '-ed' are added.

Janice was employed / emploied by the local council.

My sister always enjoyed / enjoied playing rugby.

The men carryed / carried the furniture up five flights of stairs.

The roadblock has stoped / stopped the traffic in Ponty Lane.

On Tuesday, Laurence is celebrateing / celebrating his birthday.

4) Underline the words that are spelt incorrectly below.
Then write the correct spellings out in full on the dotted lines.

worryed   smiling   ....

driving   balanceing   ....

puzzling   taking   ....

hurryed
biting   cryed   ....

Now Try This — Write down three words that follow each of these rules when you add '-ing' or '-ed':   1) change 'y' to 'i'   2) remove an 'e'   3) double a letter

Section 2 — Suffixes and Word Endings

Suffixes – 'er' and 'est'

Sometimes the spelling of the root word doesn't change when the suffixes '-er' or '-est' are added.

'perform' is the root word.   perform + -er → performer   '-er' is a suffix.

1 Add -er and -est to spell the words below correctly.

-er
old..............
few..............
small..............
tall..............

-est
old..............
few..............
small..............
tall..............

2 Add -er or -est to the sentences below so that they make sense.

Russia is cold...... than Iceland, but Antarctica is the cold...... place.

Carla is the fast...... runner at our athletics club.

Queen Lauren I is rich...... than King Michael II.

3 Add -er to spell the words below correctly.

sing..............   garden..............   teach..............

bank..............   plumb..............   wait..............

Adding '-er' to a word often turns it into a noun.

Section 2 — Suffixes and Word Endings

Sometimes the spelling of the root word changes when the suffixes '-er' or '-est' are added.

The 'e' in 'nice' disappears.

nice + -er → nicer

4 Underline the word that is spelt correctly in each word pair below.

nastyer / nastier   voteer / voter   spicyer / spicier

   tinyest / tiniest   danceer / dancer

buyer / buier   fater / fatter   easyest / easiest

5 Circle the words that are spelt incorrectly in the passage below.

Yesterday the funnyest thing happened. The manageer of our local supermarket spent hours making the floors of his shop shinyer than they had ever been before. But that afternoon a group of bikeers walked all over the shop in the muddyest boots I have ever seen.

Write the correct spellings in the box.

Now Try This Write a sentence that has a word ending in '-er' and a word ending in '-est'.

Suffixes – 'ment', 'ness', 'ful' and 'less'

Sometimes the spelling of the root word doesn't change when the suffixes '-ment', '-ness', '-ful' or '-less' are added.

'-ment' is a suffix.

'agree' is the root word. → agree + -ment → agreement

1 Draw lines from the word beginnings to the correct word endings.

Write the completed words in the box.

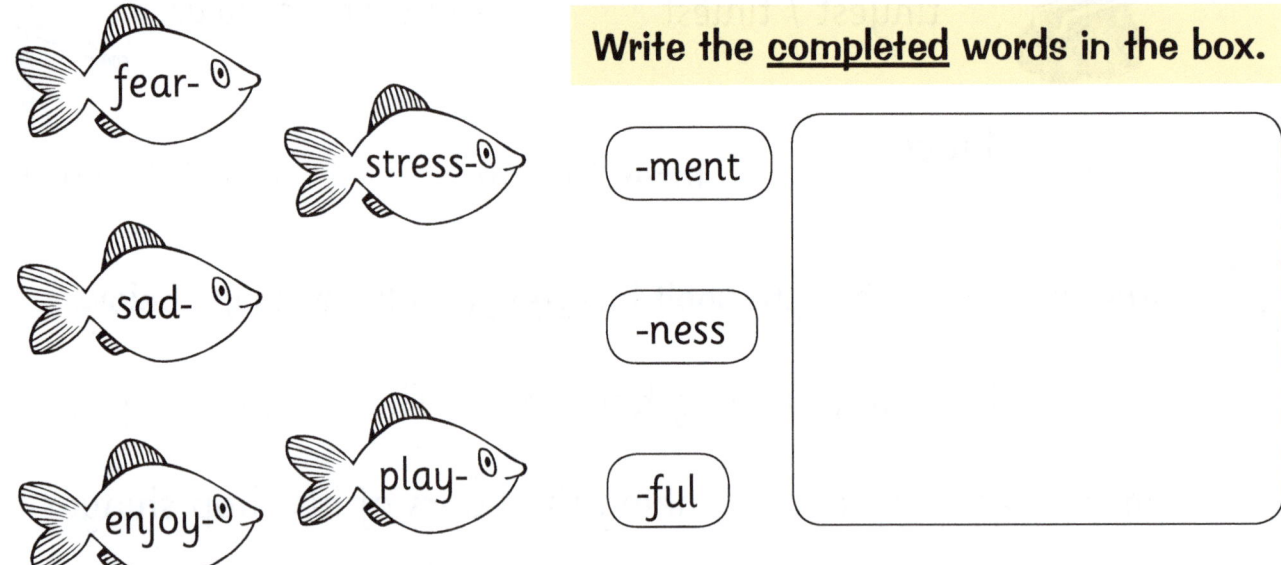

2 Complete the sentences below using the correct words from the box.

brightment / brightness   equipment / equipless

spotless / spotful

Shu cleaned the kitchen and now it looks ....

The scouts made sure they had the right ....

The seagulls were blinded by the .... of the sun.

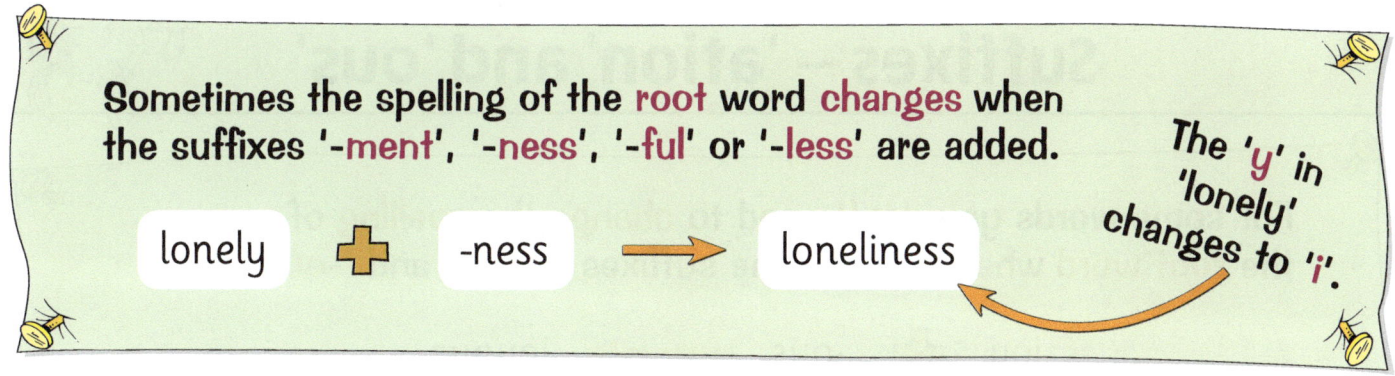

Sometimes the spelling of the root word changes when the suffixes '-ment', '-ness', '-ful' or '-less' are added.

lonely + -ness → loneliness

The 'y' in 'lonely' changes to 'i'.

3 Circle the correct spelling of each word to complete the sentences.

Lots of people think Italy is a beautyful / **beautiful** country.

I couldn't buy anything — I was pennyless / **penniless**.

It was **laziness** / lazyness that stopped me from doing his work.

We were surprised by the bumpyness / **bumpiness** of the road.

The king was mercyful / **merciful** and set the prisoner free.

Jessica's face beamed with happyness / **happiness**.

Faizal's eyes shone with merryment / **merriment**.

4 Draw lines from the words on the left to the correct words on the right.

mercy   careful / carful

easy   easyness / easiness

hope   placement / placment

care   hopeless / hopless

place   mercyless / merciless

Can you think of three root words that you can add both '-ful' and '-less' to?

Section 2 — Suffixes and Word Endings

Suffixes – 'ation' and 'ous'

For some words you don't need to change the spelling of the root word when you add the suffixes '-ation' and '-ous'.

joy + -ous → joyous

Sometimes the spelling of the root word changes when you add '-ation' or '-ous'.

The 'u' in 'humour' disappears.

humour + -ous → humorous

1 Add either -ation or -ous to spell the words below correctly.

plant + -ation → ....

fame + -ous → ....

public + -ation → ....

2 Underline the words below that are spelt incorrectly. Then write the correct spellings on the clipboard.

celebrateion

glamourous

limitation

outrageous

dangerous

locateation

relaxation

Section 2 — Suffixes and Word Endings

3) Circle the correct spelling of each word to complete the sentences.

Kelsey was busy with the party prepareation / preparation.

We are sending Qudsia an invitation / inviteation to the party.

I think that going to school on a Sunday is outragous / outrageous.

4) Add -ation or -ous to the sentences below so that they make sense.

Snowdonia is a mountain............... region in Wales.

Swimming in deep water can be danger............... .

Ali was cross that Feng had given her the wrong inform............... .

Driving in icy conditions can be hazard............... .

The hotel did not live up to Mr Butler's expect............... .

5) Use the clues to work out each word ending with -ous.

A funny joke is... → | h | | l | | | | | | |

| c | | | r | | g | | | s | ← Heroes are usually...

Superstars are often very... → | g | l | | m | | | | | |

| i | | f | | | | | | | ← Some illnesses are...

Now Try This: The suffix '-ation' turns verbs into nouns. Can you work out which verb each of these '-ation' words comes from?   creation   education   vibration

Suffixes – 'ly'

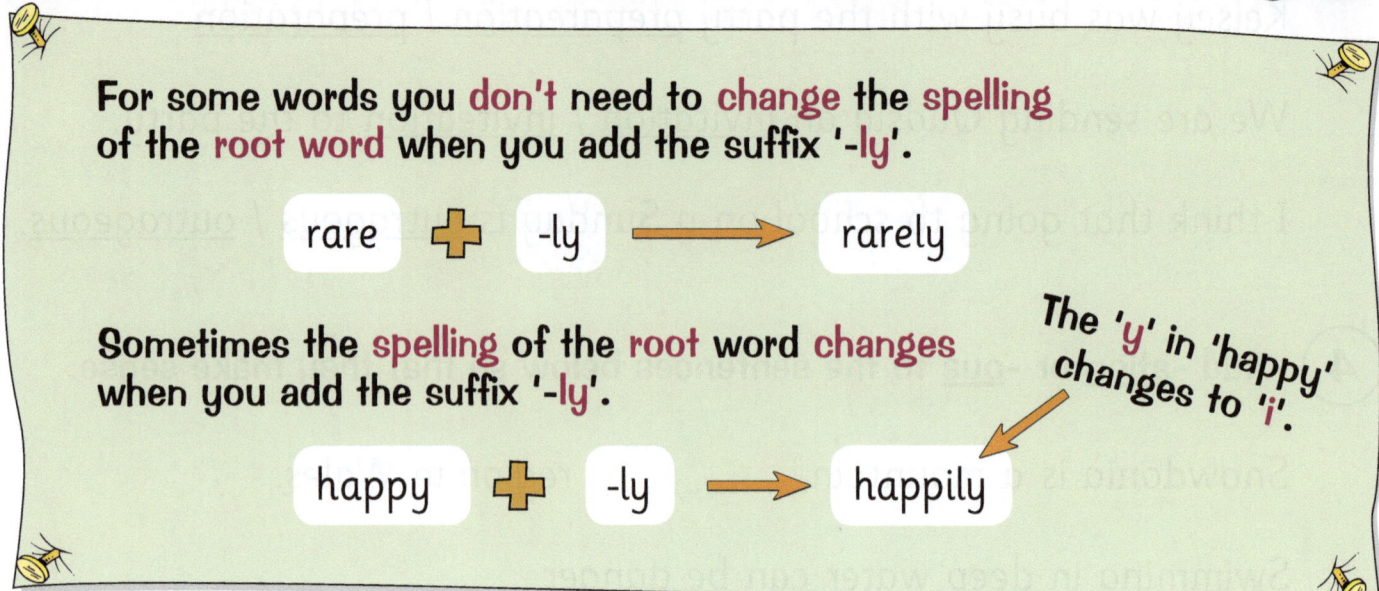

① **Add -ly to spell the words below correctly.**

angry + -ly → ....

rude + -ly → ....

simple + -ly → ....

gentle + -ly → ....

② **Circle the correct spelling of each word to complete the sentences.**

At the zoo, Mikey saw a deadly / deadily spider.

The secretary busyly / busily sorted through the post.

Mrs Fredrickson franticly / frantically searched for her car keys.

Sanjay gladly / gladily received the present from Greg.

The Queen sat nobley / nobly on her throne.

Section 2 — Suffixes and Word Endings

3) Put a tick in the boxes next to the words that are spelt correctly.
Put a cross in the boxes next to the words that are spelt incorrectly.

cuddlely ☐   boldly ☐   sensiblely ☐

badly ☐   softly ☐   calmly ☐

humblely ☐   subtlely ☐   meanly ☐

Write the correct spellings of the words you put a cross next to below.

4) Complete the sentences below using the correct words from the box.

ably / ablely   warmly / warmily   slightely / slightly

Mr Matthews .... welcomed his guests.

Paul was .... worried that Don was lost.

Pam .... completed the crossword.

5) Write as many words as you can that end in -ly on the lines below.

....

....

Now Try This — Write a short paragraph about how you get ready for school.
Use as many words ending in '-ly' as you can.

Section 2 — Suffixes and Word Endings

Word Endings – 'sure' and 'ture'

The endings '-sure' and '-ture' sound similar, but are spelt differently.

enclosure   picture

1 Draw lines from the word beginnings to the correct word endings.

pic-
mea-
ges-
na-
plea-

-sure
-ture

Write the completed words in the box.

2 Circle the correct spelling of each word to complete the sentences.

Anne thinks the enclosure / encloture is too small for the animals.

Kevin's company has started to manufacsure / manufacture fridges.

Despite the argument, I managed to keep my composure / compoture.

The witch cooked up a mixsure / mixture of slugs and snails.

The architect said the structure / strucsure was secure.

Purple Beard is searching for his lost, buried treasure / treature.

Section 2 — Suffixes and Word Endings

③ **Add either -sure or -ture to spell the words below correctly.**

lei- ➕ .... ➡ ....

tor- ➕ .... ➡ ....

crea- ➕ .... ➡ ....

④ **Sort the groups of letters below into the right order to spell a word ending in -sure or -ture.**

sure   ea   tr ➡ ....

.... ⬅ ni   ture   fur

tem   a   per   ture ➡ ....

.... ⬅ po   com   sure

ture   ven   ad ➡ ....

⑤ **Write as many words as you can that end in -sure or -ture on the dotted lines below.**

....

....

....

Now Try This Use each word from question 4 in a different sentence.

Section 2 — Suffixes and Word Endings

Section 3 — Confusing Words

The Short 'i' Sound

The **short** 'i' sound can be spelt with an **i** or a **y**.

tr**i**ck   m**y**th

1 Draw lines to show which of the words below have a short 'i' sound and which have a long 'i' sound.

nice   spill   pine   gym

short 'i'

long 'i'

wire   rapid   system   wife

2 Circle the words that are spelt correctly.

wish / wysh   tyger / tiger   chin / chyn

tyme / time   cript / crypt

3 Fill in the missing letter in each word.

…..nsect   pan…..c   g…..ft   cr…..stal

s…..rup   m…..stery   sat…..sfy   s…..nce

 List as many words containing the short 'i' sound as you can in two minutes.

The Hard 'c' Sound

The hard 'c' sound is like a 'k' sound.
Here are a few ways it can be spelt:

pri**ck**ly   **k**ing   pi**c**nic

1) The hard 'c' sounds in the words below are missing. Draw lines to match each word to its missing part.

atta?   'ck'   ?itten

wal?ing   'k'   cri?et

?offee   'c'   do?tor

2) Use the picture clues to correctly spell the hard 'c' words below.

☐☐☐☐☐☐   ☐☐☐☐

3) Use c, k or ck to complete the hard 'c' words in these sentences.

I often get homesi..... when I am away for a long time.

The o.....topus has eight tentacles.

There are 206 bones in an adult human s.....eleton.

Now Try This — Write a short passage about a football match.
Include each spelling of the hard 'c' sound at least once.

The Soft 'c' Sound

In some words, the letter c makes the soft 'c' sound. This is like an 's' sound. → cinema   place

1 Underline the words that contain a soft 'c' sound.

sentence   space   crane   excited

magic   October   pencil   create

2 Circle the words below that are spelt correctly.

grace / grase

abcent / absent

justise / justice

icy / isy

cancel / cansel

insist / incist

3 Use s or c to fill in the gaps in these words.

| s | e | n | | e |

| a | | i | d |

| d | a | n | | e |

| s | p | i | | y |

| d | e | | e | n | t |

| h | o | u | | e |

| c | h | a | | e |

| u | p | | e | t |

Now Try This Write sentences using each of the correctly spelt words in question 2.

Section 3 — Confusing Words

The 'sh' Sound

The 'sh' sound can be spelt in several different ways.

share   **s**ure   **ch**ef   mi**ssi**on

1 Use the picture clues to correctly spell the 'sh' sound words below.

......oe   para......ute   ......ugar   ......ark

2 Circle the correct spelling of each word to complete the sentences.

Jenny put her dirty clothes in the washing machine / mashine.

Amar sneezed into his tissue / tisue.

I need to buy more champoo / shampoo.

Check if it says anything about it in the broshure / brochure.

3 Complete the sentences below using the correct words from the box.

achamed / ashamed   pressure / preshure

I'm .... to say that I don't know the answer.

The .... was building as the questions got harder.

Now Try This Write down four words that contain different spellings of the 'sh' sound. Try to use words that aren't on this page.

Section 3 — Confusing Words

The 'ay' Sound

The 'ay' sound can be spelt in different ways.

mail   display   frame

1 <u>Underline</u> the words that contain an '<u>ay</u>' sound.

Try saying the words out loud to help you answer this question.

afraid   canal   brave

anyway   stare   essay   water

2 Write the <u>correct</u> spelling of each word on the dotted lines.

saylor    graypes    calculaite

....

3 <u>Find</u> the words with '<u>ay</u>' sounds in the wordsearch.

translate   faint
plane   waist
bake   clay
behave   Monday
paid   always
nail   dismay

 Write three sentences, using as many words from question 3 as you can.

Word Families

Word families are groups of words that contain the same root. Their meanings are related — like a family.

All of these words contain the root 'act'. They are all about doing something.

action   active   react

① **Underline** the words that belong to the same word family as frost.

frosting   lost   decline   frostbite

define   frosted   defrost   bitten

② Draw lines to match each word to the box that contains a word from the same family.

deface		trustworthy
	face	
distrust		movement
	move	
preface		facing
	trust	
remove		trusted

③ Write two more words for each of the word families below.

take / mistake ➡ ....

date / dating ➡ ....

do / redo ➡ ....

 Think of four words that belong to the same family as each of these words: 1) luck   2) play   3) form

Section 3 — Confusing Words

Plurals

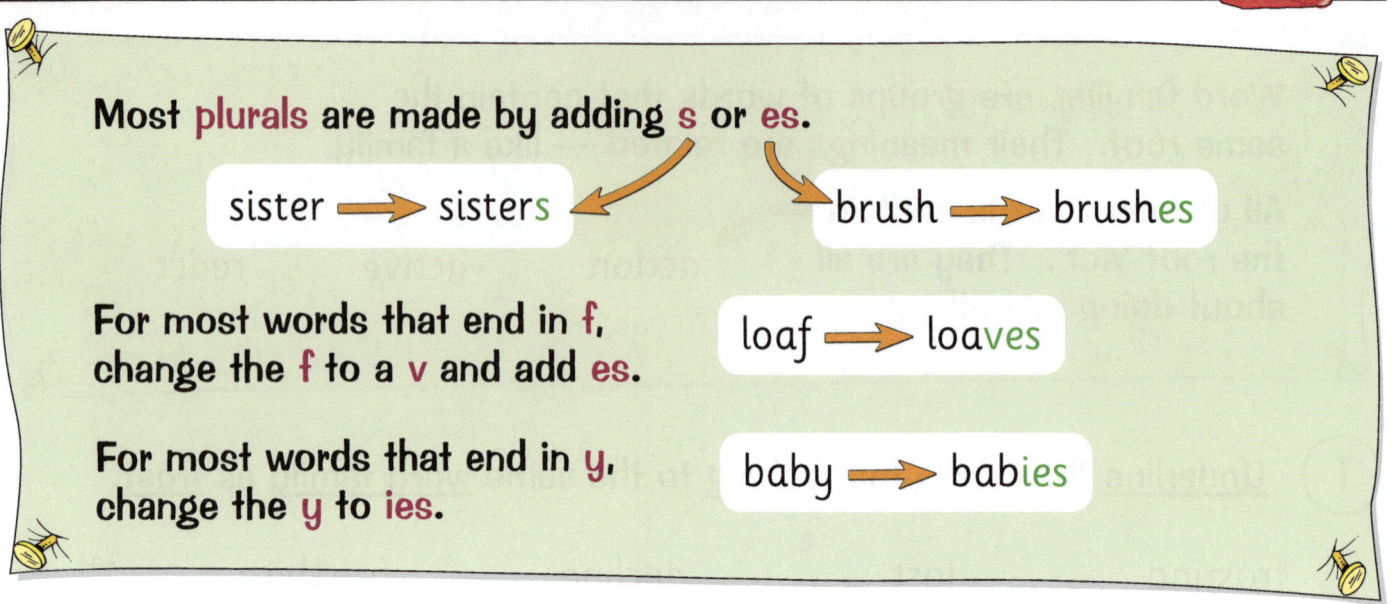

Most plurals are made by adding s or es.

sister → sisters   brush → brushes

For most words that end in f, change the f to a v and add es.

loaf → loaves

For most words that end in y, change the y to ies.

baby → babies

1) Add <u>s</u> or <u>es</u> to each of these words to make them plural.

church......   piano......   key......

potato......   box......

2) These plurals are spelt <u>incorrectly</u>. Write the <u>correct spelling</u> of each.

ponys →		wolfs → ....
leafes →		thiefs → ....
difficultys →		apologys → ....
shopes →		shelfs → ....
torchs →		foxs → ....
bucketes →		penciles → ....

Section 3 — Confusing Words

Some plurals don't follow the rules. You just have to learn these.

sheep ➡ sheep   foot ➡ feet   child ➡ children

3) Complete the table below.

Word	Plural
goose	....
mouse	....
reflex	....
elf	....
woman	....

4) Finish these sentences by writing the plural of the words in brackets.

I always clean my .... (tooth) before bed.

My aunt split the cake into two .... (half).

The rock climbers saw the .... (cliff) as a challenge.

5) Write the plural of each of these words in a sentence.

donkey ➡ ....

sandwich ➡ ....

batch ➡ ....

Now Try This — Can you write a sentence that includes plurals ending in 's', 'es' and 'ies'?

Possessive Apostrophes

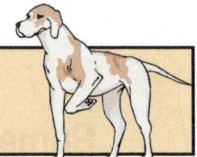

Possessive apostrophes show that something **belongs** to someone.

Jim's dogs → The dogs **belonging** to Jim.

You don't need an apostrophe to show that a word is **plural**.

1) Cross the phrases which use apostrophes <u>incorrectly</u>.

Adjoa's dad ☐   Peter's kitten's ☐   Gemmas' bat ☐

Elsa's shoes ☐   Jeremys' pens ☐   Adrian's ball ☐

Rewrite the <u>incorrect</u> phrases with <u>apostrophes</u> in the <u>correct</u> places.

_____

2) <u>Underline</u> the words in the passage that are <u>missing</u> apostrophes. Then <u>rewrite</u> the words with the <u>correct apostrophes</u>.

Dear Sura,

Please come to Judiths party tomorrow. We are going in Mums car. She is taking me and Matts sister, so there will definitely be room for you and Jackies cake. Bring Kevins playing cards as well.

....
....
....
....
....

Section 3 — Confusing Words

'It's' is a shortened form of **'it is'** or **'it has'**.

It's raining ⟶ It is raining.

The word **'its'** means **'belonging to it'**.

Its paw ⟶ The paw belonging to it.

The word **'its'** never has a possessive apostrophe.

3 Use either <u>its</u> or <u>it's</u> to <u>complete</u> the sentences below.

.... your turn to do the washing-up.

The gorilla beat .... chest to scare .... rival.

Mr Chen's cat ate all of .... food straight away.

4 <u>Rewrite</u> the phrases below using a <u>possessive apostrophe</u>.

The rabbit belonging to my sister ⟶ ......My sister's rabbit......

The ship belonging to the pirate ⟶ ....

The mop belonging to the cleaner ⟶ ....

5 <u>Write</u> sentences using <u>possessive apostrophes</u> with each of the words below.

grandma ⟶ ....

Thomas ⟶ ....

parrot ⟶ ....

Now Try This: Find five objects that belong to different people. Write a list of the objects, using possessive apostrophes to show who they belong to.

Section 3 — Confusing Words

Homophones

Homophones are words that sound the same, but have different **meanings** and **spellings**.

bury — To bury something is to cover it completely.

berry — A berry is a small fruit. E.g. raspberry

1 Write the homophone that matches each picture.

main → ....

be → ....

bare → ....

son → ....

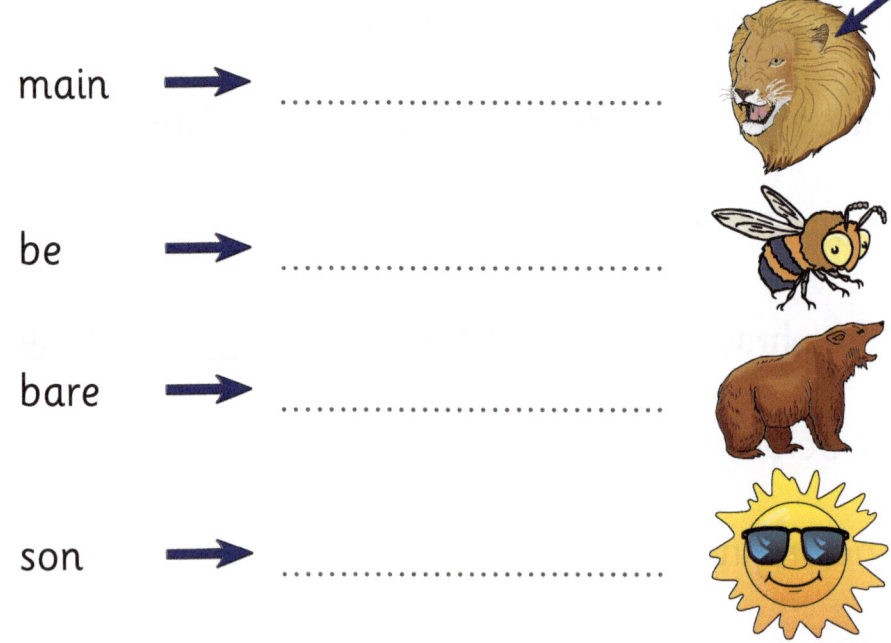

2 Circle the correct spelling of each word to complete the sentences.

Vegetarians don't eat meet / meat.

Where shall we meat / meet?

I can't accept / except this.

I like all vegetables accept / except carrots.

Don't brake / break anything.

Make sure you brake / break at the corner.

Section 3 — Confusing Words

3 Fill in the gaps in these sentences using the correct words from the box.

> there   their   they're

Becky and Habiba dyed .... hair the same colour.

Are .... any biscuits left in the tin?

Three people said .... coming to my party.

4 Find a homophone for each of the words below. Then find all of the words in the wordsearch.

sea → s | e | e

reign → r | a | |

here → h | | a |

dear → d | | | r

maid → m | | | e

```
O W E R D E E R
R B A E E W D A
L M A I D L I L
A E O G T N S W
D R H N S S E E
E H E R E T A Y
A M A D E R Y S
R N R A I N T E
```

5 Write each of these words in a sentence.

to → ....

two → ....

too → ....

Now Try This Can you write a sentence that uses all of the homophones in question 3?

Section 3 — Confusing Words

Section 4 — Mixed Spelling Practice

Mixed Spelling Practice

1) Split the words below into prefixes and root words.

unpaid → .... + ...

subcategory → .... + ...

mistrust → .... + ...

recycle → .... + ...

2) Add the suffixes to the words below and then write the words out in full.

busy- +
- -er → ....
- -est → ....
- -ing → ....
- -ed → ....

happy- +
- -est → ....
- -ly → ....
- -er → ....
- -ness → ....

3) Circle the words that are spelt incorrectly. Write the correct spellings on the dotted lines.

antisocial   submarine   information

merryment   usualy   disimilar

angryly   picsure   superglue

....
....
....
....

4) The <u>hard</u> '<u>c</u>' sound in each word below is missing.
Draw lines to <u>match</u> each word to its missing part.

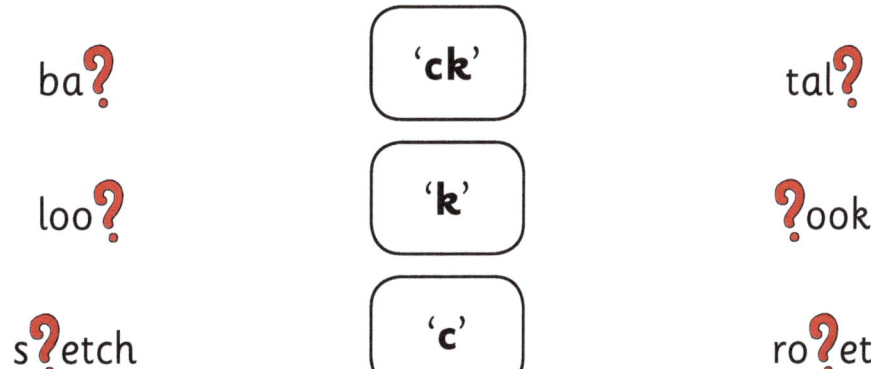

5) Circle the <u>correct</u> spelling of each word to <u>complete</u> the sentences.

The detective promised to look into the <u>mistery</u> / <u>mystery</u>.

When we go skiing, we stay in a <u>shalet</u> / <u>chalet</u>.

I can't lift that <u>weight</u> / <u>waight</u>.

Tim needed to find a cash <u>machine</u> / <u>mashine</u>.

<u>Thay</u> / <u>They</u> are going on holiday next month.

The <u>mith</u> / <u>myth</u> was fascinating to learn about.

6) <u>Complete</u> the <u>table</u> below.

Word	Plural
country	....
box	....
thief	....
potato	....

Section 4 — Mixed Spelling Practice

7) Cross the phrases which use apostrophes incorrectly.

Andys' hat ☐   Ayse's mum ☐   Ruths' mug ☐

Lily's cat's ☐   Taran's pencil ☐   Sam's dogs ☐

8) Solve the clues to complete the crossword.

Across

1. Connects your head to your shoulders.
2. To behave badly.
3. One less than twice.
4. Magicians perform these.

Down

1. The person who lives next door.
2. A tunnel under a road.

9) Write each pair of homophones in a sentence.

sail / sale → ....

....

I / eye → ....

....

Spelling Hints and Tips

Spelling can be quite tricky. Here are some hints and tips to help you spell the words that you find most difficult.

1. **Break** the word up into **smaller** parts.
   e.g. ex-**per**-i-**ment**   par-**tic**-u-**lar**   im-**por**-tant

2. Make up a **sentence** to help you remember how to spell the word.
   e.g. **possess**   **P**irates **O**ften **S**ail **S**hips **E**ncountering **S**tormy **S**eas

3. Look for **smaller words** within the word.
   e.g. h**ear**t   not**ice**able   cour**age**ous
   You could make a sentence with both words in to help you remember.
   e.g. Harry told a **lie** and now I don't bel**ie**ve him.

4. If there's a word that you find **particularly difficult**, try writing it out **correctly** and then **copying** it out lots of times. When you think you know it, try **covering** up the correct spelling and seeing if you can get it right **without looking**.

If you get really stuck, try these tips to help you work out the correct spelling.

1. Remember other words that follow the **same rule**.
   e.g. happy + **ness** = happiness
   lovely + **ness** = loveliness

2. Think about words that **sound the same**.
   e.g. th**ough**t   br**ough**t   f**ough**t

3. Think about different ways that **similar sounds** can be spelt.
   e.g. ti**ck**   **k**itten   **c**at

Spelling Hints and Tips

Answers

Section 1 – Prefixes

Pages 4 and 5 – Prefixes – 'un', 'dis' and 'mis'

1. un + known
   mis + print
   dis + approve
   un + even

2. unaware
   unequal
   disregard
   unpaid
   misbehave

3. You should have underlined: **diskind**, **discalculate**, **unspell** and **misappoint**. The correct spellings are: **unkind**, **miscalculate**, **misspell** and **disappoint**.

4. disown, mistreat, mismatch, dismiss, displease, disagree

5. **un**well
   unlocked
   disappeared
   misunderstood
   unpacked

Page 6 – Prefixes – 're' and 'anti'

1. **anti**clockwise, **anti**septic, **re**charge, **re**fresh, **re**write, **anti**climax, **re**create, **re**heat, **re**design

2. reapply, antibiotic, reopen, antivirus, resend, return

Page 7 – Prefixes – 'sub' and 'super'

1. submarine
   superglue
   supermarket
   superhero

2. **sub**merge
   supersonic
   subdivided
   subheading

3. Any correctly spelt words that start with the correct prefixes. Examples:
   supervision, supersize, superpower, superstar
   sublet, sublevel, subtotal, subtitles

Section 2 – Suffixes and Word Endings

Pages 8 and 9 – Suffixes – 'ing' and 'ed'

1. hunting, hunted
   jumping, jumped
   treating, treated

2. perform**ing**
   entertain**ed**
   deliver**ing**

3. shopping
   struggling
   employed
   enjoyed
   carried
   stopped
   celebrating

4. You should have underlined: **worryed, balanceing, hurryed, cryed**. The correct spellings are: **worried, balancing, hurried, cried**.

Pages 10 and 11 – Suffixes – 'er' and 'est'

1. older, fewer, smaller, taller
   oldest, fewest, smallest, tallest

2. cold**er**, cold**est**
   fast**est**
   rich**er**

3. sing**er**, garden**er**, teach**er**, bank**er**, plumb**er**, wait**er**

4. nastier, voter, spicier, tiniest, dancer, buyer, fatter, easiest

5. You should have circled: **funnyest, manageer, shinyer, bikeers, muddyest**. The correct spellings are: **funniest, manager, shinier, bikers, muddiest**.

Answers

Answers

Pages 12 and 13 – Suffixes – 'ment', 'ness', 'ful' and 'less'

1. **fearful**, **sadness**, **enjoyment**, **stressful**, **playful**

2. **spotless**
   equipment
   brightness

3. **beautiful**
   penniless
   laziness
   bumpiness
   merciful
   happiness
   merriment

4. mercy — **merciless**
   easy — **easiness**
   hope — **hopeless**
   care — **careful**
   place — **placement**

Pages 14 and 15 – Suffixes – 'ation' and 'ous'

1. plant**ation**
   fam**ous**
   public**ation**

2. You should have underlined: **celebrateion**, **glamourous**, **locateation**.
   The correct spellings are: **celebration**, **glamorous**, **location**.

3. prepar**ation**
   invit**ation**
   outrage**ous**

4. mountain**ous**
   danger**ous**
   inform**ation**
   hazard**ous**
   expect**ation**

5. hilari**ous**
   courage**ous**
   glamor**ous**
   infecti**ous**

Pages 16 and 17 – Suffixes – 'ly'

1. angrily
   rudely
   simply
   gently

2. deadly
   busily
   frantically
   gladly
   nobly

3. You should have ticked: **boldly**, **badly**, **softly**, **calmly**, **meanly**.
   You should have crossed: **cuddlely**, **sensiblely**, **humblely**, **subtlely**.
   The correct spellings are: cudd**ly**, sensib**ly**, humb**ly**, subt**ly**.

4. warmly
   slightly
   ably

5. Any words ending in -ly that are spelt correctly.
   Examples:
   smoothly, **quietly**, **loudly**, **proudly**

Pages 18 and 19 – Word Endings – 'sure' and 'ture'

1. picture, measure, gesture, nature, pleasure

2. enclosure
   manufacture
   composure
   mixture
   structure
   treasure

3. leisure
   torture
   creature

4. treasure
   furniture
   temperature
   composure
   adventure

Answers

5. Any words ending in -sure or -ture that are spelt correctly.
   Examples:
   closure, **unsure**, **assure**, **ensure**, **pressure**, **reassure**
   capture, **feature**, **posture**, **nurture**, **culture**

Section 3 – Confusing Words

Page 20 – The Short 'i' Sound

1. Words with a short 'i' sound: **spill**, **gym**, **rapid**, **system**
   Words with a long 'i' sound: **nice**, **pine**, **wire**, **wife**
2. w**i**sh, t**i**ger, ch**i**n, t**i**me, cr**y**pt
3. **i**nsect, pan**i**c, g**i**ft, cr**y**stal, s**y**rup, m**y**stery, sat**i**sfy, s**i**nce

Page 21 – The Hard 'c' Sound

1. atta**ck**, wal**k**ing, **c**offee, **k**itten, cri**ck**et, do**c**tor
2. **c**astle, du**ck**
3. homesi**ck**
   o**c**topus
   skeleton

Page 22 – The Soft 'c' Sound

1. **sent**en**ce**, **spa**ce, ex**c**ited, pen**c**il
2. gra**c**e, ab**s**ent, ju**s**ti**c**e, i**c**y, **c**an**c**el, in**s**ist
3. **s**ense, a**c**id, dan**c**e, spi**c**y, de**c**ent, hou**s**e, cha**s**e, up**s**et

Page 23 – The 'sh' Sound

1. **sh**oe, para**ch**ute, **s**ugar, **sh**ark
2. ma**ch**ine
   ti**ss**ue
   shampoo
   bro**ch**ure
3. a**sh**amed
   pre**ss**ure

Page 24 – The 'ay' Sound

1. **afraid**, **brave**, **anyway**, **essay**
2. **sailor**, **grapes**, **calculate**
3.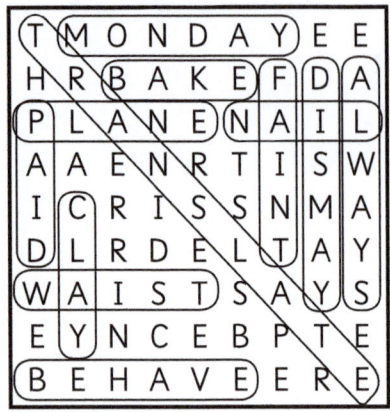

Page 25 – Word Families

1. **frosting**, **frosted**, **defrost**, **frostbite**
2. face: **deface**, **preface**, **facing**
   move: **remove**, **movement**
   trust: **distrust**, **trustworthy**, **trusted**
3. Any correctly spelt words from the correct word family.
   Examples:
   taking, **retake**
   dated, **outdated**
   doing, **undo**

Pages 26 and 27 – Plurals

1. church**es**, piano**s**, key**s**, potato**es**, box**es**
2. pon**ies**
   lea**ves**
   difficult**ies**
   shop**s**
   torch**es**
   bucket**s**
   wol**ves**
   thie**ves**
   apolog**ies**
   shel**ves**
   fox**es**
   pencil**s**

Answers

3. geese
   mice
   reflexes
   elves
   women

4. teeth
   halves
   cliffs

5. Any sentence containing the correct plural.
   Examples:
   The **donkeys** were tired after their long journey.
   We had ham **sandwiches** for lunch.
   I baked three **batches** of cookies.

Pages 28 and 29 – Possessive Apostrophes

1. You should have crossed: **Peter's kitten's**, **Gemmas' bat**, **Jeremys' pens**
   The correct phrases are: Peter's kitten**s**, Gemma**'s** bat, Jeremy**'s** pens

2. You should have underlined: **Judiths**, **Mums**, **Matts**, **Jackies**, **Kevins**
   The correct spellings are: Judith**'s**, Mum**'s**, Matt**'s**, Jackie**'s**, Kevin**'s**.

3. **It's** your turn to do the washing-up.
   The gorilla beat **its** chest to scare **its** rival.
   Mr Chen's cat ate all of **its** food straight away.

4. the pirate's ship
   the cleaner's mop

5. Any sentences that use possessive apostrophes correctly.
   Examples:
   My grandma's name is Jeanne.
   Thomas's football kit was very dirty.
   The parrot's claws were very sharp.

Pages 30 and 31 – Homophones

1. mane
   bee
   bear
   sun

2. Vegetarians don't eat **meat**.
   Where shall we **meet**?
   I can't **accept** this.
   I like all vegetables **except** carrots.
   Don't **break** anything.
   Make sure you **brake** at the corner.

3. Becky and Habiba dyed **their** hair the same colour.
   Are **there** any biscuits left in the tin?
   Three people said **they're** coming to my party.

4. You should have written:
   rain, **hear**, **deer**, **made**

5. Any sentence where the word is used correctly.
   Examples:
   I am going **to** Oxford.
   There are **two** sides to the argument.
   I like that one **too**.

Section 4 – Mixed Spelling Practice

Pages 32 to 34 – Mixed Spelling Practice

1. **un + paid**
   sub + category
   mis + trust
   re + cycle

2. **busier, busiest, busying, busied**
   happiest, happily, happier, happiness

Answers

3. You should have circled: **merryment**, **usualy**, **disimilar**, **angryly**, **picsure**
   The correct spellings are: **merriment**, **usually**, **dissimilar**, **angrily**, **picture**

4. ba**ck**, loo**k**, **sk**etch, tal**k**, **c**ook, ro**ck**et

5. **mystery**
   chalet
   weight
   machine
   They
   myth

6. **countries**
   boxes
   thieves
   potatoes

7. You should have crossed:
   Andys' hat
   Ruths' mug
   Lily's cat's

8. Across:
   1. **neck**
   2. **misbehave**
   3. **once**
   4. **tricks**
   Down:
   1. **neighbour**
   2. **subway**

9. Any sentence where the words are used correctly.
   Examples:
   I went to a **sale** and bought a **sail**.
   I have a problem with my left **eye**.